Majestic Splendor

JAN BURTON

CrossHouse

CrossHouse Publishing
2844 S. FM 549
Suite A
Rockwall, TX 75032
www.crosshousebooks.com

© 2011 by Jan Burton
All rights reserved.
Printed in the United States of America

No part of this publication may be reproduced, stored in a retrieval system, or transmitted in any form or by any means—electronic, mechanical, photocopying, recording, or otherwise—without the prior written permission of the publisher.

Unless otherwise indicated, all Scripture taken from the Holy Bible, New Living Translation, © 1996, 2004, 2007 by Tyndale House Foundation. Used by permission of Tyndale House Publishers, Inc., Carol Stream, Illinois, 60188. All rights reserved.

ISBN: 978-1-61315-019-1

Library of Congress: 2011942677

Table of Contents

Preface 5
Nurses 7
Surrendered Heart 9
Paradise 11
Unfamiliar Ground 13
Fulfill His Promises 15
Diamonds in Rough 17
Midst of the Storm 19
Earthquake in Haiti 21
Unique Potential 23
Walking in Season 25
Greater Things 27
Pressures of Life 29
Abandoned Praise 31
The Father's Love 33
Godly Character 35
Christian Hunger 37
Ordinary People 39
Giants Shall Fall 41
God's Instruction 43
It's My Season 45
Teach Me, Lord 47
Searching for People 49
The Battle 51
Gate to Salvation 53
Motions 55
Jesus Condemned 57
God's River 59
Sweet Aroma 61
Love of God 63

In Christ	65
Greater Love	67
Arm of the Lord	69
Leaders	71
Marriage is a Gift	73
Position Established	75
Answered Call	77
Gracious	79
Bond Us Stronger	81
Measure of Faith	83
Our Creator	85
Restoration	87
Savior Who Saves	89
Holy Ghost	91
The Savior Walked	93
The Wilderness	95
Master Plan	97
Hungry for God	99
Rustic Mission	101
Real Worship	103
Jesus, Our Conduit	105
Majesty	107
Judgement	109
Faith	111
Life is Sweet	113
Your Journey	115
Team Complete	117

Preface

This collection of poems is the next level in my Christian journey. The natural eye cannot see the supernatural things of God. My prayer for you is to be encouraged in the faith and step out into the deeper waters and experience His majestic splendor.

Jude 25—"All glory to him who alone is God, our Savior through Jesus Christ our Lord. All glory, majesty, power, and authority are his before all time, and in the present, and beyond all time! Amen."

—*Jan Burton*

John 3:16

For God loved the world so much that he gave his one and only Son, so that everyone who believes in him will not perish, but have eternal life.

Nurses

Nursing is the venue
God chooses to work through
Predestined by God to serve
Our profession He has reserved

Our path of service
The Lord has designed
Sharing His love with the world
That none is undone and left behind

Hearts filled with compassion
The nurse's hands He has blessed
The touch of the Savior
Brings healing and rest

Matthew 24:42

*So you too, must keep watch!
For you don't know what day
your Lord is coming.*

Surrendered Heart

Is your heart surrendered?
Given Jesus your all?
Holding nothing back
What He has promised you shall not lack

One day He is coming
He is asking, "Are you ready?"
It will be a glorious day
Live your life as if it were your last day

Sometimes things happen in ways we don't want
Who are we to question?
We can't seem to understand why
Just know it's part of God's plan for our life

He knows where we're going
We've stayed upon His path
Obedience to do what He commands
Departing not from His perfect plan

God is in charge of our life
It is not our own
Our destiny He controls
When tests come, we will
Come out pure as gold

Revelation 21:2

And I saw the holy city, the new Jerusalem, coming down from God out of heaven like a bride beautifully dressed for her husband.

Paradise

In the Paradise of God
Stands the tree of life
To him that overcomes
Receives the crown of life

To eat of the tree
One has borne good fruit
The Lord knows
Passionate souls with deep roots

Lord, You have created
All things by Your hand
For Your good pleasure
As innumerable as the grains of sand

Clothed in white raiment
One day we'll be around that throne
Singing praise and hallelujahs
To the Lamb wearing crowns of gold

Beyond the crystal sea
It shimmers like glass
The covenant of our God
We shall see at last

What a day that will be
Because we are made for Paradise
To enter the gates
For our names
Are written in the Lamb's Book of Life

Psalm 24:8

Who is the King of glory?
The Lord, strong and mighty;
the Lord, invincible in battle.

Unfamiliar Ground

As we walk over unfamiliar ground
God scatters our enemies like chaff
For we are never alone
Be strong, for I AM
The First and Last, who sits on the throne

The armor is the ammunition
Defending the Word of God
All the parts must fasten together
Victorious living is all that matters

Lord God, Creator of all earth
Who knew me before my birth
No one can snatch me out of Your hand
Redemption received by the blood of the Lamb

The Lord my God is coming
Yes, He comes in all power
There is none equal to Him
His arm rules like a strong and mighty tower

Daily strengthening His flock
Carrying us on His wings
Holding us close to His heart
He promised to never depart

Psalm 145:13

*For your kingdom is an everlasting kingdom.
You rule throughout all generations.
The Lord always keeps his promises;
he is gracious in all he does.*

Fulfill His Promises

God will fulfill His promises
All provisions He will make
In our weakness we are strong
To You, the Holy One, we hold on

Jesus is the lifeline
The anchor that holds
To your rescue He'll come
Showing the way back home

God will use whomever He wants
Knowing generations past and future
Bringing His purpose to fruition
Sharing the gospel through the Great Commission

Keeping His promises
Delivering always in time
Forever You are faithful
Trustworthiness makes us not doubtful

Representing You in the world
Preaching the Word of God
Saved from sin's grasp and death
Victory is ours throughout eternity
In the Kingdom that never ends is certainty

Isaiah 26:7

*But for those who are righteous,
the way is not steep and rough.
You are a God who does what is right,
and you smooth out the path ahead of them.*

Diamonds in Rough

Diamonds in the rough
Edges He makes smooth
Unlimited with God's connection
When our hearts are vertical to You

People are like flowers
Get old and wither away
Our God never changes
He stays the same always

God's Word is eternal
Constant and unfailing
It needs no help standing alone
His grace outflows at the throne

Guidance and solutions
To every problem or need
Instructions are in the Bible
Just open the Word, finding answers as you read

Come to the Lord
He has all we'll ever need
To live a full life
As man He has set free

The Body of Christ
Each has a part to play
Grow us up in holy faith
Imitating You, Lord, every day

Proverbs 3:5-6

*Trust in the Lord with all your heart;
do not depend on your own understanding.
Seek his will in all you do, and he will
show you which path to take.*

Midst of the Storm

In the midst of the storm
We know God is in control
Peoples' lives are in His hands
This day He knew before man

The Lord is ever present in our time of need
He is always waiting for us to ask
Our prideful ways are strong
We tend to seek Him last

Run to the Lord
Trust in Him with all your might
Hold on to Jesus
Pressing on in the fight

Encourage one another
Lifting up your sisters and brothers
Precious child of God you are
Thoughts of you do not escape the Lord's mind
Move on forward, leaving the past behind

The Lord is our provider and supplier of all we need
Just put your faith in Him and believe

Matthew 24:7-8

*Nation will go to war against nation,
and kingdom against kingdom.
There will be famines and earthquakes
in many parts of the world.
But all this is only the first of the birth pains,
with more to come.*

Earthquake in Haiti

A powerful earthquake in Haiti occurred
Your warning was not only felt, but heard
Awaken souls of people to be stirred

People buried underneath the rubble
The living and dead
Their lives before their eyes have crumbled

Bodies stacked on the ground
Mass graves had been dug
The stench of death is all around

Lord, outstretch Your healing hand
Mending their hearts full of pain
Restore back their lives and land

Those who are left open their eyes
Prophesy is being fulfilled
This is no surprise

How many departed this life
Dead to sin, not having everlasting life

Proverbs 4:11-12

*I will teach you wisdom's ways
and lead you in straight paths.
When you walk, you won't be held back;
when you run, you won't stumble.*

Unique Potential

Every child of God has unique potential
Following His steps is sequential
Walking the path that is straight and narrow
Divinely ordained with purpose and power

Living the extraordinary life
Success You bring holds no strife
Plugged to the power source
Directing toward the heavenly course

Challenges will arise
None that can't be overcome
Our past prepares for the future
Steadfastly holding to the Lord's love

Trusting in our inner voice
Sitting silent to hear
Quicken our spirits
To hear directions for the new year

Prayer opens the doors
Communicating thoughts to the Lord
Meditating day and night
The desires of our heart He delights

Help us, Lord, to observe
Every truth hidden in Your Word
Making the way prosperous
In all we have heard

Ecclesiastes 3:1

*For everything there is a season,
a time for every activity under heaven.*

Walking in Season

Walking in our season
In authority, power, and prosperity
Receiving the blessing and promises
Going with expectations out of the ordinary

Marriage is a covenant of love
Together we are joined as one
Complementing each other's strengths
Where one is weak, the other is made strong

Submission is the key to obedience
An act of the heart
The husband is the head over the wife
The body of Christ has many parts

Mold me, make me
Body, mind, spirit, soul
Christ is the Church
Master and ruler of the universe

John 14:12

I tell you the truth, anyone who believes in me will do the same works I have done, and even greater works, because I am going to be with the Father.

Greater Things

Greater things done in Jesus' name
Glory to the Lamb, blessing the holy name
Declaring the Word of the Lord
Completing every assignment sending us for

Standing at the throne of grace
Whatever it takes to worship and praise
Blotting out the noise
Positioned to hear Jesus' voice

True worship changes the atmosphere
Relentless prayer to persevere
Just a praise away
What God can do today

Equipping for greater destiny
Our minds cannot perceive
Appointed and anointed
Through the power of the Holy Trinity

God's spoken Word represents authority
No one can deter my future
Circumstances turn around
Confident of the calling, I'm heavenward bound

1 Peter 1:6

*So be truly glad.
There is wonderful joy ahead,
even though you have to endure
many trials for a little while.*

Pressures of Life

When pressures of life come
Not knowing which way to go
Press into prayer
Tarrying to receive the answer Jesus holds

As the fierce winds blow
Pushing our way through
Waiting patiently
Until we receive word of what to do

So don't lose heart
God heard my cry
The miracle you need
Won't pass you by

Trust God with your praise
He will divinely intervene
While walking through the wilderness
Upon the everlasting arms we lean

Everything the devil stole
We fight to take it back
Spiritual weapons our arsenal
Giving the enemy no slack

The trials of life
Cause us to stand strong
Having done all
Jesus is still on the throne

Ephesians 1:6

*So we praise God for the glorious grace
he has poured out on us
who belong to his dear Son.*

Abandoned Praise

Praise uninhibited
As the anointing flows
Supernatural things happen
Deeper into reverence we go

Pouring over and into each
Filling the atmosphere with praise
Losing ourselves in worship
All the rest of our days

God holds each
In the palms of His hands
Godly character is woven
Developing qualities of integrity in man

Citizens of the heavenly kingdom
God's destiny surely comes to pass
Enemies cannot scatter
God's promises that outlast

A life marked by change
Moving from grief to glory
Like a beautiful butterfly
Transformed by God's superiority

1 John 3:1

*See how very much our Father loves us,
for he calls us his children,
and that is what we are!
But the people who belong to this world
don't recognize that we are God's children
because they don't know him.*

The Father's Love

The Father's love is matchless
His grace permeates my soul
When the Master's hand touched me
He healed me and made me whole

Motivated by God's sovereign love
A merciful God is He
Goodness He always brings
Spiritual blessings we cannot see

God holds us to a higher standard
Study to show thyself approved
Sharing the word of truth
His Holy Spirit works in hearts to be moved

Romans 5:4

*And endurance develops strength of character,
and character strengthens
our confident hope of salvation.*

Godly Character

Godly character is required
Leading to holiness, therefore,
The steps of a man or woman
Are ordered by the Lord

Grown into this character
We are destined to become
Remade from the inside out
By the shedding of Jesus' blood

Walk upright in the Holy Spirit
Do what is pleasing unto the Lord
Maturing our character
Knowing what our purpose is for

Sold out to God
Knowing Whose we are
Pursuing and pleasing
With all our heart

Carrying the anointing
Living by God's power
He is ruler and reigns
Transforming His children hour by hour

Revelation 3:20

*Look! I stand at the door and knock.
If you hear my voice and open the door,
I will come in, and we will share
a meal together as friends.*

Christian Hunger

When Christians hunger
We're fed a diet of God's Word
Full of His nourishment
The heart is stirred

Sensitive to the Spirit inside
Prompting to seek God's face
Feeling the touch of His presence
Giving us more grace

Vessels of the Lord
Wholly and completely His
Our closets must be cleansed
Purifying us daily from our sins

Jesus said, "Come, sup with me."
You're invited to dine at the table
Growing and thriving
Achieving greatness at insurmountable levels

Matthew 19:26

Jesus looked at them intently and said, "Humanly speaking, it is impossible. But with God everything is possible."

Ordinary People

God uses ordinary people
Just like you and me
Doing extraordinary things
Only that His eyes can see

Jesus is our precedent
Following demands obedience
Faith produces endurance
Pure vessels to serve is our assurance

Jehovah is God of the impossible
Magnificent is His wisdom
His calm brings stability
Developing character releases ability

Fit for the Master's use
Discipline cultivates testing
Prayer leads into the heavenly realm
Persistent faith can touch Jesus' hem

God's peace set us apart
Step out of the old
Venture into the new
Greater potential released through you

Romans 12:21

*Don't let evil conquer you,
but conquer evil by doing good.*

Romans 8:37

*No, despite all these things,
overwhelming victory is ours
through Christ, who loved us.*

Giants Shall Fall

Now's the time giants shall fall
Let us not stay safe, holding back
Look unto God, for He is bigger
Coming into our greatness, being delivered

Hardships we face with tribulations
Conquering fears
Driving out our foes
Victoriously chanting our cheers

Train us for battle
Giving wisdom with keen insight
Responding quickly with obedience
Avoiding situations that cause plight

In hard or difficult times
We experience further preparation
God equips us with elements
Moving us to a higher elevation

So don't be afraid
Stand strong, keeping watch
God's almighty hand is with us
The enemies' camp He will blotch

How loving You are, God
Always faithful and true
Showing Your mighty power
Working good in every situation, trusting You

Joshua 1:8

*Study this Book of Instruction continually.
Meditate on it day and night so you will be
sure to obey everything written in it.
Only then will you prosper
and succeed in all you do.*

God's Instruction

Stepping out on God's instructions
Brings results of His blessing
The blessing can come to us today
Associating with others He sends our way

Redeemed from the curse of law
Entering in to salvation and promises of God
Connected to Christ through Abraham's seed
God provides resources and provisions we need

God's divine seeds sowed
Govern success and prosperity
No matter where we go
The coat of blessing brings overflow

Speak well of others
Sow greater than yourself
Moving upward, not down
Financially you'll reap gaining ground

Choices He allows
Are we going to hear and obey?
Harvested seeds will multiply blessings
Written in the Word of God today

Joshua 1:7

*Be strong and very courageous.
Be careful to obey all the instructions
Moses gave you. Do not deviate from them,
turning either to the right or to the left.
Then you will be successful in everything you do.*

It's My Season

Everything the Lord does has a reason
2009—it is my season
Test and trials produce genuine faith
There is no compromising nor debate

Keeping our eyes on the prize
Veering not to the right or left
Promises we have not imagined
To be revealed unto us yet

Let us not be restrained
Enjoying the fruit of our labor
How can we not trust You, Lord?
Pursue us with Your love
When we are faithful, You open doors

Psalm 143:10

*Teach me to do your will,
for you are my God.
May your gracious Spirit
lead me forward on a firm footing.*

Teach Me, Lord

Teach me, Lord, to see through Your eyes
That my spirit will be sensitive to hearts that are blind

Teach me, Lord, to hear with Your ears
Deliver Your messages that have become clear

Teach me, Lord, to speak with Your voice
The words You give according to Your choice

Teach me, Lord, to love, give, and feel with Your heart
With Your biblical principles You impart

Teach me, Lord, to teach and heal with Your hands
It's by Your Spirit and power released unto man

Teach me, Lord, to walk with Your feet
That my heart will be lowly and meek

2 Chronicles 16:9a

*The eyes of the Lord search the whole earth
in order to strengthen those
whose hearts are fully committed to him.*

Searching for People

The Father is searching for people
From east to west
Willing to obey and serve
Wholeheartedly giving more and not less

All having a purpose to complete
We are one of a kind
Created uniquely for You
Made by Your special design

Build character, integrity in each life
Take us out of the way
Our audience of one
The everlasting God to whom we pray

Orchestrate our steps
Not laboring in vain
Mature us in faith
Strength we will gain

We are the same in God's eyes
New challenges are arising
Whether we are red, yellow, black, or white
We are precious in His sight

Whom will you serve today?
Be still and listen
Hear what the Lord
Of the harvest has to say

2 Chronicles 32:8a

*He may have a great army,
but they are merely men.
We have the Lord our God to help us
and to fight our battles for us!*

The Battle

In the battle the Lord fights for us
Don't whine or complain
Watch His mighty hand rescue and deliver
Arrows fly to the adversary from His quiver

When we feel trapped
Seems there is no way out
Jesus is moving us around
Where we need to be
Closing in the gap

Spare us, oh Lord, from grief
Our suffering not worthy to be compared
It's just a light affliction
We are going through
A spiritual process to attain our breakthrough

Prepare us for the next issue we face
Getting past anxiety and fear
With confidence we shall overcome
Conquering in the future a greater frontier

It's time to get moving
Taking action, trusting God to open the way
Stand still so the world will know
I am your God
My glory in you will be displayed

John 10:9

*Yes, I am the gate.
Those who come in through me will be saved.
They will come and go freely and will find
good pastures.*

Gate to Salvation

Jesus, You're the gate to salvation
The way, the truth, and the life
There's no other way to come into the kingdom
Receive His grace and He will give you freedom

Taste His living water
Jesus said you will never thirst again
Those who are weak
Come to the fountain for a drink

Jesus, You're the source of all life
His love is unlimited
He is our safety and security
Transforming us with holiness and purity

Victory and power over death You gave
As You ascended to Heaven from the grave

Titus 1:16

*Such people claim they know God,
but they deny him by the way they live.
They are detestable and disobedient,
worthless for doing anything good.*

Motions

Are people just going through the motions?
No private time with the Lord or devotion
Taking up a space on the pew
The gate to Heaven is narrow
To enter will be few

Are they wearing a mask?
Looking good on the outside putting on a show
Making others think they believe
Their hearts are corrupt and only deceive

In the world they live like hell, but fake at church
Living life full of sin
Nobody can hide themselves from Him
Lord, send conviction upon them
Through the Holy Spirit to invite Your presence in

Denomination or religion won't make it right
Only a personal relationship with Jesus Christ

John 3:17

God sent his Son into the world not to judge the world, but to save the world through him.

Jesus Condemned

Jesus was condemned
To die upon the cross
His atonement for our sins
Cleansed our hearts from within

The truth has set us free
From darkness to His wondrous light
The power of Satan's grip to God
Through the blood of Jesus Christ

Delivered from all condemnation
The mind purged and conscience cleared
Self and sin have died
Our life in Christ make alive

Overwhelm us, Lord,
With Your holy presence
Source of our life
How majestic is Your name
The everlasting light

Revelation 22:1

Then the angel showed me a river with the water of life, clear as crystal, flowing from the throne of God and of the Lamb.

God's River

God, how great is Your river?
How deep and long does it run?
Quench my thirst
With the Father, Spirit, and Son

Drinks You give of living water
To be abundantly satisfied
Deeper knowledge You reveal
How we are cherished, and You glorified

To know the love of the Father
How You love us so
All children of the nations
This You desired them to know

Amazing is Your love
The Holy Spirit so strong
Powerful is Your presence
Among Your people You will be made known

Hebrews 13:15

Therefore, let us offer through Jesus a continual sacrifice of praise to God, proclaiming our allegiance to his name.

Sweet Aroma

Lord, reveal Your will and Your way
May we be a sweet-smelling aroma to You every day

Your joy floods my soul
My future in Your hands You hold

Voices You give to sing
Praise with one voice we bring

Guard our hearts and minds
In Your will keep us aligned

We must rejoice in the good and bad
Whether we are glad or sad

Lavish Your love down
To reach souls once lost but now found

With Your love You lead us home
One day face to face we'll meet at the throne

Ephesians 3:18-19

*And may you have the power to understand,
as all God's people should, how wide,
how long, how high, and how deep his love is.
May you experience the love of Christ,
though it is too great to understand fully.
Then you will be made complete with
all the fullness of life and power
that comes from God.*

Love of God

There is no end to the love of God
It is limitless and has no boundaries

It runs deeper than the deepest well
The love of the Father forgives even when we fail

It reaches higher than the eye can see
To the highest mountain beyond its peak

It is longer than can be measured
The love of Christ is our treasure

It is wider than our mind can perceive
The mystery of Christ is within you and me

1 Peter 2:9

*But you are not like that, for you are a
chosen people. You are royal priests,
a holy nation, God's very own possession.
As a result, you can show others the
goodness of God, for he called you
out of the darkness into his wonderful light.*

In Christ

In Christ, I am a princess
A royal heir to the king
Seated with the worthy Lamb
Bowing before Him to the ground

Forerunner for Jesus You left me to be
A chosen vessel to carry Your word as You see
His jewel and special treasure
Beauty in the eyes of the Lord cannot be measured

Who am I but His daughter
How I love You, my heavenly Father
Child of God by Your redeeming grace
Secure in You, Lord, by my faith

John 15:1-2

*I am the true grapevine, and my Father
is the gardener. He cuts off every branch
of mine that doesn't produce fruit,
and he prunes the branches that do bear fruit
so they will produce even more.*

Greater Love

Father, Your love is greater than any other
Amazing is Your grace
Nothing here on earth can compare
We are going to a better place

Great passion and love You have bestowed
Teaching us to love with the Father's heart
As Your servant, Lord
Your will be done as You impart

We are the branches
Jesus, You are the vine
Bearing fruit from the tree of life

The harvest is ready
Good seeds we plant
Eternal life Jesus gives
The spirit of the believer forever lives

Psalm 44:3

*They did not conquer the land
with their swords; it was not their own
strong arm that gave them victory.
It was your right hand and strong arm
and the blinding light from your face
that helped them, for you loved them.*

Arm of the Lord

The arm of the Lord is strong
It upholds us when things go wrong
Mercy and grace He gives
Renew us daily for You as we live

Our strength is in Jehovah Jireh
In our weakness He provides the strong tower
When the enemy tries to rise
Under our feet he will go with his lies

Lord, strengthen our souls
That we will become bold
Broken spirits You revive
The Spirit of the Lord is alive

The Lord is our Salvation
He is the ruler of all the nations
For every purpose, there is a plan He works through
His children have great expectations of all
He is going to do

Matthew 20:26-28

But among you it will be different. Whoever wants to be a leader among you must be your servant, and whoever wants to be first among you must become your slave. For even the Son of Man came not to be served but to serve others and to give his life as a ransom for many.

Leaders

Godly leaders are willing to sacrifice
Time, money, even our family cannot get in the way
God has to be first place
All the obstacles that hinder He can erase

Think about His love
When He died for you and me
Freeing us from the grip of sin
Dying on a tree at Calvary

Lord, only You can satisfy
Staying connected to the vine
So our grapes
Will not cast before their time

While our life on earth is short
Let us bear good fruit
In all deeds we shall do
Lord, everything is accountable to You

Christians are held to a higher standard
Excellency the Lord deserves
Every task should be completed with enthusiasm
On the journey as we serve

Hebrews 13:4a

Give honor to marriage, and remain faithful to one another in marriage.

Marriage is a Gift

Marriage is a gift from God above
Man and woman He created
Giving us helpmates to cherish and love

Beginning with a new start in life
Two hearts are joined as they come
Christ is the center that unites us as one

Love is always patient and kind
It waits upon God to send that special one we find
The future ahead, the past behind

Built upon the principle of love
Filling their home with joy and bliss
Their wedding vows are sealed with a kiss

God's love is a banner and guide
Their dwelling and children will be blessed
Bonding them together with peace and rest

Whom God this day has brought together
Husband and wife they are forever

Ephesians 1:3

All praise to God, the Father of our Lord Jesus Christ, who has blessed us with every spiritual blessing in the heavenly realms because we are united with Christ.

Position Established

Father, the Maker of Heaven and earth
Conversion brought us rebirth
Sins of the old man died
Christ Jesus made us alive

Our position is established
God's Word is written on tablets
Sons and daughters of the Most High
Branches abiding in the true vine

An advocate we have with the Father
Bulls and goats we no longer have to offer
Jesus is our source of life
Confess our sins, no longer living in strife

Learning through failure brings success
Abiding in our position, Jesus brings rest
Brothers who are weakened
Our experiences help them to be strengthened

Boldly coming to the throne of grace
His mercy we need to stay in the race
All things work together for our good
God the Father has understood

Isaiah 55:11

*It is the same with my word.
I send it out, and it always produces fruit.
It will accomplish all I want it to,
and it will prosper everywhere I send it.*

Answered Call

Father, our team answered Your call
To be flexible, adaptable, tolerable above all
The task You sent us to do
No language barrier inhibited glorifying You

The seed You provided
Led us on the path Your hand guided
Upon arrival, some had no luggage or bins
The lesson taught us to be content within

Every day we entered camp, the children waved
Anticipating their smiling faces made our day
Games we played and songs we sang
Each day amazing increase You gave

Extra time one day
After finishing our crafts, Lord, You made
Prayers You answered to reach the unsaved
Your timing is always perfect and never late

The Holy Spirit's prompting sent forth Your word
Void it would not return as the children heard
Accomplishing all You sent it to do
Twenty Ukrainian children accepted You

Our mission would be complete
Reflecting the Savior for these people to meet
Divine encounters our eyes did see
Manifestations of Your Spirit supernaturally

Psalm 50:10

For all the animals of the forest are mine, and I own the cattle on a thousand hills.

Gracious

God is so gracious to me
Even to depths that I cannot see
God has promised He will make a way
He remains by my side every day

We go through times when God is silent
He is still in control, for He is the pilot
We listen closely to hear His voice
Often it's just a whisper above the noise

Lord, teach and show me the way
Things about You I've never imagined in these days
Draw me nearer and closer than before
Opening doors to experience Your love even more

God is able to provide the means
The cattle He owns are fat and not lean
Speak to hearts to sow their seeds
One day in Heaven all the faces they will see

Ecclesiastes 4:12

A person standing alone can be attacked and defeated, but two can stand back-to-back and conquer. Three are even better, for a triple-braided cord is not easily broken.

Bond Us Stronger

Husband and wife together You have joined
Bond us stronger in Your love as one
Take us deeper within
As the mystery of Your love unfolds and begins

While on our journey show us the way
Our destiny You gave on our wedding day
We can't thank You enough or even have the words to say
As we count the many blessings You give each day

Our lives are out in front of us
Lord, You are faithful and You we trust
The road may not always be easy
Let our sacrifices for You be well pleasing

Your grace reaches to places unknown
Even to the high and low
You, Father, are our bread alone
The riches of Your love You want all to know

Matthew 17:20b

*I tell you the truth, if you had faith
even as small as a mustard seed,
you could say to this mountain,
"Move from here to there,"
and it would move.
Nothing would be impossible.*

Measure of Faith

A measure of faith
You have given to each
Some are strong, yet some are weak
Messengers of the gospel word, we preach

The love of Christ You placed in each heart
You said You would never leave us nor part
In order to receive
You have got to believe

His grace is for the humble
We give of ourselves to You
You gave Yourself for us
As You saw us through the cross

How excellent is His name
Higher than the angels above
The trees bow down before Him
His name means love

1 Peter 4:19

So if you are suffering in a manner that pleases God, keep on doing what is right, and trust your lives to the God who created you, for he will never fail you.

Our Creator

God, our Creator
Provider of all we need
You are Jehovah Jireh
Overflowing love You bring

Faith is not in man's wisdom
Purge us of our sin
But the power of God
Acknowledging and submitting to Him

The Lord God is our judge
Of all we have done wrong or right
One glad day we'll stand
With our lives displayed before His sight

May we be found worthy
Of everything He would have us to say and do
For He Who is faithful
Abounds His grace to you

2 Corinthians 12:9

*"My grace is all you need.
My power works best in weakness."
So now I am glad to boast about
my weaknesses, so that the power of Christ
can work through me.*

Restoration

Looking back to where we have been
Now is the time to live and begin
To give God our best
His grace is sufficient when we rest

Awaken Your people to watch and pray
Restore souls with new beginnings today
Move us into new dimensions
Bringing different times and seasons You mentioned

Life is too precious and short
For those who make serving You their last resort
Redefine each to Your plan
We are here to serve You and not man

Father, give us a fresh touch
While embracing the new
Transforming our hearts to be more like You

Ephesians 2:8-9

God saved you by his grace when you believed. And you can't take credit for this; it is a gift from God. Salvation is not a reward for the good things we have done, so none of us can boast about it.

Savior Who Saves

Jesus, You overcame the world
Despite the suffering and pain
So all mankind would come to know
The Savior who saves

The gift of salvation is free
His mercy and grace has no cost
It's open to all
Forgiveness of sin He gives to the lost

Open your heart
Ask Him to enter in
He longs to give you
A new life with Him

Eternal life He has promised
To all who believe
Jesus took our place on the cross
As He died for you and me

Matthew 3:11

"I baptize with water those who repent of their sins and turn to God. But someone is coming soon who is greater than I am—so much greater that I'm not worthy even to be his slave and carry his sandals. He will baptize you with the Holy Spirit and with fire.

Holy Ghost

Thank the Lord the most
We can do nothing on our own
It's only by His strength
Because He filled us with the Holy Ghost

He makes His ministers a flame of fire
The anointing of God they carry
Sanctified by the Word of God
Until Jesus Christ tarries

Nourished by words of faith
Saturated in prayer to God
The living God who gives all things
To His imminent presence we cling

As we brought nothing into this world
It is certain we'll carry nothing out
Righteousness and godliness we follow after
Laying hold of life now and eternally thereafter

Hebrews 12:2

We do this by keeping our eyes on Jesus, the champion who initiates and perfects our faith. Because of the joy awaiting him, he endured the cross, disregarding its shame. Now he is seated in the place of honor beside God's throne.

The Savior Walked

To the cross the Savior walked
As He hung there the people watched
Soldiers played for His clothes, casting lots

The veil ripped, He died
It was finished
The work He came to do was done
God said, "This is My beloved Son."

Into the tomb, His body placed to stay
The soldiers became afraid, scared away
On the third day
He arose from the grave

Death and hell He overcame
The blood of the Lamb was slain
Our victory in Jesus is His fame

Isaiah 43:19

For I am about to do something new.
See, I have already begun! Do you not see it?
I will make a pathway through the wilderness.
I will create rivers in the dry wasteland.

The Wilderness

The voice of the Lord is silent
Traveling through the wilderness
We must trust in You, Jehovah
Times of testing bring readiness

Unveil our eyes to see the truth
Are we indeed weak or strong?
The devil's tempting tries our faith
Luring us, hoping we will do wrong

The Lord has won the battle
He has spoken over His child
Obey, doing whatever I say
Die to yourself, crucifying the flesh today

Deeper roots are grounded to the source
Fountains will spring up
Quenching our thirst
New breakthroughs outwardly burst

Planted near the river
Our branches are watered
The vine equips with all we need
Flourishing us like an olive tree

Jeremiah 29:11

"For I know the plans I have for you," says the Lord. "They are plans for good and not for disaster, to give you a future and a hope."

Master Plan

God has the master plan
He unfolds it one step at a time
When we give our life to Him
We surrender ourselves to glorify Him

We are a chosen race
To live a holy life
Proclaiming His excellency
In a world not living right

Help us, Lord, find our place
We are a people of faith
In Your shadow, I'll fear no evil
For You are with me covered by grace

God, You are my Father
Adopted into the family
The keys to the kingdom given to me
Going to release and set the captives free

When God calls
He expects us to respond
Where do you fit in God's plan today?
Commit your life, submit without delay

Matthew 5:6

God blesses those who hunger and thirst for justice, for they will be satisfied.

Hungry for God

Intensely hunger for the things of God
Thirst for His very presence
Drawing and moving closer through His Word
Listening carefully accepting the answer heard

Your Word I esteem more than my food
Sustain and feed my body spiritually
Your Word is spirit and life
In my body there is unity and no strife

Incline my ear to Your understanding
Submiting and obeying
God's Word is medicine to my flesh
In Your Spirit, Lord, I find rest

My soul pants after Thee
I look for You, Oh God
Show me Your power and glory
Let me be still, not in a hurry

Early I will seek You
Let me eat what is good
Lord, You satisfy my soul
Out of my belly shall rivers flow

Made in God's image
Created for His divine purpose
Fellowship with God in His essence
The fullness of joy is in His presence

Luke 14:23

So his master said, "Go out into the country lanes and behind the hedges and urge anyone you find to come, so that the house will be full."

Rustic Mission

A rustic mission in Africa
To the bush of Karuma I traveled
A team of women and men combined
In pod houses we slept and dined

The orphans greeted us with songs
While the workers in the fields laid bricks
Behind us was the beautiful Nile River
Where Moses was found and delivered

Medical clinics were held for days
People walked from far distances away
Worms in their bellies, scabies on their skin
The blood of Jesus healed them within

One hundred souls were saved
One young girl in particular
She ran to my side, fell on her knees
She said, "I want Jesus to save me."

Many prayed the sinner's prayer
Even in my sickness while there
Jesus gave me the strength
To hold on and keep going
Completing my assignment at great lengths

New relationships were formed
Women, men, and children were reborn
Jesus was the gateway to healing the torn
The people of Uganda are being restored

John 4:23-24

But the time is coming—indeed it's here now—when true worshipers will worship the Father in spirit and in truth. The Father is looking for those who will worship him that way. For God is Spirit, so those who worship him must worship in spirit and in truth.

Real Worship

The Father is seeking worshippers
Who worship in spirit and truth
Anyone can sing a song
Be born again through the blood-washed throng

Worship the Word of God
Not what man may say
The aroma going through the motion stinks
Be for real, it only matters what God thinks

You cannot worship with sin in the heart
Repent, and be free
Worship comes from deep within
Be in love with the Lord
The Word of God is our sword

God is omnipresent
He hears and sees all
True worship is loving God
When He comes, His glory is revealed
Cast your light to shine
Upon your face His glory is divine

Ephesians 3:20

*Now all glory to God, who is able,
through his mighty power at work within us,
to accomplish infinitely more than
we might ask or think.*

Jesus, Our Conduit

Jesus, You are the Conduit
Giving keen insight and wisdom
As we plug into Your plan
Not into the worldly ways of man

Jesus is a God of connections
People He places in our paths
The Word is our training manual
Living righteously, not in His wrath

Enhancing our walk
Trusting and obeying
Move on with God
Listen to what He has to say

There is great power in the Word
Coming from the Great High Priest above
Our ears and hearts must be attentive
Our soul is purchased by His blood

Don't forget any of His benefits
We are entitled to them all
Perseverance is the key to His call

Psalm 96:6

Honor and majesty surround him; strength and beauty fill his sanctuary.

Majesty

Reveal Your Majesty
Glorious splendor in the skies
I see fire burning in Your eyes

Without Your loving grace
Life here is just a vapor
Our walk is at a champion's stride
To be a champion, You run the race

Focus on the Master's work
Taking charge of my very thoughts
Your Will is my desire
Everything is in my heart

Cover my face with Your glory
People don't have to ask
The kindred spirit; they just know

My eyes must stay straight on course
At the end of my life
I want to hear, "Well done."
There shall be no remorse

Hebrews 12:1

Therefore, since we are surrounded by such a huge crowd of witnesses to the life of faith, let us strip off every weight that slows us down, especially the sin that so easily trips us up. And let us run with endurance the race that God has set before us.

Judgement

Judgement begins at the house of God
Follow the foundation already laid
Get rid of the hindrances
So you'll be in a desirable place

God looks at our houses
What cleaning needs to be done?
Smoothing out the rough spots
Removing the garbage and all sin's blots

When life seems to be a fog
We've sometimes gone our own way
God can clear our eyes
Forgiveness of sin we no longer hide

Remove every idol
That seems to trip us up
Align our behavior
To be a sweet-smelling savor

Jesus is waiting
For some banners to be raised high
Held to His standards
The Word is truth and cannot lie

Walk in the appropriate manner
His Word is our bond
Focused on what's most important
It has joined us to Him as one

James 2:17

*So you see, faith by itself isn't enough.
Unless it produces good deeds,
it is dead and useless.*

Faith

Faith is an action word
It causes you to move
Will you sit or stand?
Faith always follows through

Live for God
Because you believe
If you do nothing, faith is dead
Are you standing on the Word He has said?

When God is for us
Who can be against us?
If God says you can
You don't have to be afraid of man

Faith takes the risk
Get out of the zone
Don't stay the same
If you do, things will never change

Break free of your fears
Go for your dreams
Where there is liberty
There freedom rings

When God makes a deposit
He expects a return
Go on pressing forward
Using the tools you have learned

Proverbs 3:5-6

*Trust in the Lord with all your heart;
do not depend on your own understanding.
Seek his will in all you do, and he
will show you which path to take.*

Life is Sweet

Life is sweet
Quit wasting so much time
Run to God
He holds His arms open wide

Are you empty inside?
He'll fill you up with His holy presence
Begin releasing the pain
Healing you will gain

If you have been hurt
All the wounds He will heal
Peace inside will come
Scars remain, but wounds are sealed

When troubled, yet not despaired
Trust in Jesus, for your life He cares
Listen to be shown His will
With the fruit thou shall be filled

God places people in our path
That have suffered the same circumstance
Those godly encounters He brings
For He is glorified in His body
For He has done great things

John 15:16-17

*You didn't choose me. I chose you.
I appointed you to go and produce lasting
fruit, so that the Father will give you
whatever you ask for, using my name.
This is my command: Love each other.*

Your Journey

Live out your journey
Having no regrets
Time is passing quickly
Are you giving your best yet?

Will you serve the Lord?
Give over your entire heart
Do not withhold anything
Submit every part

Do whatever God tells you
Live His Word day in and day out
Make yourself a drink offering
Pleasing and poured out

Burn up this flesh
That stands in the way
Bear good fruit
That stays and remains

Go through the process
Walk in God's favor
Position yourself to trust Him
In His eyes, you are a precious gem

Life is like a dash
Here today, gone tomorrow
What are you going to do that will outlast?

Ephesians 6:11

Put on all of God's armor so that you will be able to stand firm against all strategies of the devil.

Team Complete

Our team complete with seven
Was the message received from Heaven
Yet another change God made
He added one youth to make it eight

Each chosen by God
To accomplish His perfect plan
Reaching the lost and saved—
Even those who know Him, but have strayed

Kids living in inner city projects
Starving for love and affection
Where drugs, alcohol, and violence are present
Causing their children to feel rejection

A wandering woman totally dismayed
Came to children's camp asking for some change
She asked our pardon for drinking her beer
Only Jesus can quench her thirst—that He made clear

She stood in need of prayer
Concerning marriage problems she was having to bear
Prayed she would turn her life around
To the only One where peace is found

Sometimes God uses simple things
To lead a person to Christ
One soul came into the Kingdom
Panama Park is where He received freedom

The enemy tried to defeat us
By making our ankles swell
Every day the armor was on as the Lord prevailed
Victory was ours as the enemy failed

Ministering to body, soul, and spirit
The love of Christ we showed
Leaving an impact upon their lives
Jesus loves them more than they know

Numbers 6:24-26

May the Lord bless you and protect you.
May the Lord smile on you and be gracious to you.
May the Lord show you his favor
and give you his peace.

www.ingramcontent.com/pod-product-compliance
Lightning Source LLC
Chambersburg PA
CBHW030330080526
44584CB00012B/799